What Your Cat Really Thinks

Other Titles by Susan McMullan

Hamish McHamish of St Andrews
Keep Calm and Get a Cat
Dog Shaming: Canine Confessions!

What Your Cat Really Thinks

Susan McMullan

BLACK & WHITE PUBLISHING

First published 2014
by Black & White Publishing Ltd
29 Ocean Drive, Edinburgh EH6 6JL

1 3 5 7 9 10 8 6 4 2   14 15 16 17
ISBN: 978 1 84502 652 3

The publisher has made every reasonable effort to contact copyright holders of images
in this book. Any errors are inadvertent and anyone who for any reason has not been
contacted is invited to write to the publisher so that a full acknowledgment can be
made in subsequent editions of this work.

A CIP catalogue record for this book is available from the British Library.

Designed by Creative Link, North Berwick
Printed and bound in Poland
www.hussarbooks.pl

In loving memory of Mrs Margaret MacNaughton. A kind-hearted lady who was always full of fun and laughter and was never afraid to say what she really thought!

Introduction

They say dogs believe they are human while cats believe they are God. Independent, poised, aloof and confident – they keep us all wrapped around their adorable little paws while we pander to their every whim.

But what if you could tell exactly what your fluffy feline was thinking? What if you could delve into their minds and hear what they really thought of the world . . . and of you? Now you can! What Your Cat Really Thinks shares the adorable photographs of cat worshippers from all over the world who know that, while their cuddly kitties might look cute and innocent, looks can be deceiving!

Think your lovable companion enjoys seeing you come home at the end of a long, hard day? Convinced that your treasured tabbies sit on your lap because you're the apple of their eye? Don't be fooled!

This book is a celebration of man's other best friend. So sit back and relax as you share in the highs and lows of being owned by a cat. But be warned! Your cherished moggie might not be thinking what you'd expected!

I don't often pose for the camera.
But when I do, I nail it.

All those expensive cat toys and my favourite thing in the whole wide world is this brown paper bag.

DEAL WITH IT.

5

TODAY THIS TWIG. TOMORROW THE WORLD.

FOR THIS you will pay.

This is what I think of your conversation.

You are a thief of joy.

A great big thief of joy.

Don't worry. Today I'm going to make the most of all the

16 MINUTES

I'm awake.

For the love of God. Will you please stop getting changed when we're in the room?

AND YOU WONDER WHY
THE OTHER CATS WON'T
LET ME PLAY?

I've had enough:

it's **ME** or the dog.

I sit here because it's warm.

NOT BECAUSE I LIKE YOUR COMPANY.

Case in point:
never agree to a blind date.
NEVER.

I LICK MY BUM and then I KISS YOUR FACE.

Don't hate the player, hate the game.

I'm not blocking the view. I am the view.

JUST CHILLING.
You should try it some time, you uptight son of a gun.

Forget about them - they just pay the mortgage.

This is our house.

Bring me some popcorn, human servant. I'm watching a chick flick.

You've gotta help me get through to this mutt. Cat kebab is not on the menu!

Seriously, you're wearing that?

This may look like your bed.
And you may like to call it your bed.

BUT IT'S ALL MINE.

No rush, just FYI - **we missed the litterbox.**

Our favourite place to poop will always be your pillow.

You were right. Never eat yellow snow.

I've seen how many **PHOTOS YOU HAVE** of me on your Facebook page.

YOU ARE FAR TOO CLINGY.

It wasn't me. I didn't do it.
You can't prove anything.

I found it! Another home for the dog.
THIS IS HAPPENING.

Bum in your face. Cos that's how I roll.

OMG! Humans are so ugly.

Sleeping peacefully?
Time for me to
ATTACK YOUR FEET.

This is my 'do not disturb' pose.
RESPECT MY WISHES.

This would be a whole lot more fun if I was still alive.

Remember I know all your secrets. Now take a left or I'll tell everyone.

That cute little baby voice you use when you talk to me?

Not. A. Fan.

I'M IMAGINING YOUR HEAD BETWEEN MY PAWS. AND NOT IN A GOOD WAY.

Take it from me. You don't want to know what just happened here.

ARGH! SOMEBODY GET ME
TO THE NAIL SALON. QUICK!

Disturb me if you dare.

Goodbye, beautiful home.

HELLO,

shredded furniture.

Thank goodness you're home.
Someone **POOPED** in the sink.

You and me?
WE NEED TO HAVE WORDS.

Not on my to-do list today? Spending time with you.

Idiot friend.
Everyone has one.

IS THERE AN

OWNER ADOPTION SERVICE?

Sometimes seeing you just ruins my whole day.

Cat hair on everything?

MY WORK HERE IS DONE.

Everything tastes better with cat spit in it.

Honest.

Does this look like the face of a cat that wants to watch football again?

Your cooking is the pits.
You need to take a long
hard look at yourself.

You will pay me some attention.
You will.

SHAPE UP HUMAN!

Crunches are for pussies.

That whole 'blame your farts on me' thing is so last year.

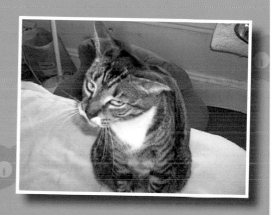

POINT THAT CAMERA AT ME ONE MORE TIME . . .

I'm hiding here for a reason:
TO GET AWAY FROM YOU.

Little do you know that this is my walk of shame.

It's not what you said.

It's the way you said it.

YUP.

I'm a cat on a mat. Go figure.

Dolly was right - working nine to five ain't no way to make a living.

If you were going for pantomime couture then yes, your make up looks great.

Some people are

TRYING TO SLEEP,
you know.

The fashion police called. They want to speak to you about your outfit.

We regret nothing.
NOTHING.

We are going to scratch everything you own.

Who's awesome?

We're awesome.

You on the other hand ?
Let's just say we're still undecided.

We are way too cool to be your friends.

There aren't many things **MORE ANNOYING** in my nine lives than you.

This behaviour has got to stop. Me and my box need our privacy.

Give me my treats now or the **sofa gets it.**

Night vision is awesome. This pooch has no idea what I have planned.

I'm not going anywhere with you.
I have street cred to maintain.

See?
This is what living with you does to me.

YEAH, WE'RE TROUBLE.
You looking for us?

Your breath is terrifying.

Being your friend is so boring.

HOW DID I END UP WITH YOU?

Yup, I'm moody and unpredictable.
Like looking in the mirror, isn't it?

I was wrong about you
getting a hobby.

WE NEED to find
you a new boyfriend.

I wish you'd listen to yourself talk.
Then maybe you'd stop.

Can I have some help here, please?

MY OPINION OF YOUR OPINION.

I AM A GENIUS.

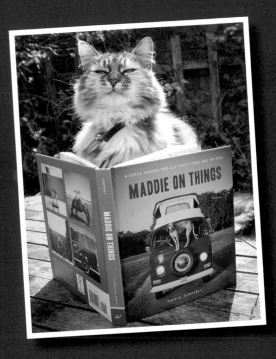

You, however, got me a book about a dog.

I'd pretty much do anything not to have to look at you right now.

Take it from me -
THE LESS YOU KNOW
about this situation
THE BETTER.

I don't enjoy exercise. Just about as much as I don't enjoy your company.

Well my food bowl isn't going to fill itself is it?

It's true, I'm adorable. Keep telling yourself that when I meow in your ear at 4am.

You're telling me I have to live here forever?
Where is the
COMPLAINTS DEPARTMENT?

You make me want to

scratch out

my own eyes.

Cool is my middle name.
Stick that in yer pipe and smoke it.

I am indeed **VERY BEAUTIFUL.**
Shame I can't say the same about you.

The last thing the dog remembers seeing.

Of course I'm in shape.
ROUND IS A SHAPE.

We'd really
APPRECIATE
it if you wore
PANTS MORE OFTEN.

I have claws and I'M NOT afraid to use them.

I know I say this a lot but
I DO NOT
remember doing that.

Acknowledgements

Special thanks to Steven Barker who allowed me to use his photograph of his much-loved cat Willow. A true character and a joy to have around, Willow is dearly missed.

Credit is due to the following people for kind permission to use their photography. Names are provided in the order that the photographs appear.

Marion and Cameron Murray

Kerry Clark

Meg Price

Kevin McMullan

Tjarko Busink

Carol Ramsay

Gill Ballie

Kristi

Liz

Kerry Kydd

Clint Jaysiel

Tjarko Busink

Frances Pratt

Jared Pellegrini

Steven Barker

Gill Ballie

Kerry Kydd

Kerry Kydd

Jill Slater

Lee-Ann Patterson

Claire McLellan

Kerry Kydd

Kerry Clark

Frances Pratt

Sergey Nechaev

Grace Rajaretnam

Lee-Ann Patterson

Alexey Chernov

Chiaki Higashino

Lee-Ann Patterson

Kevin McMullan

Imajane: http://www.flickr.com/photos/insanejane

Kevin McMullan

Meg Price

Steven Barker

Steven Barker

Steven Barker

Ela Kowalczyk

Steven Barker

Hody Deavers

Alison Hutchison

Will Haas

Claire McLellan

Harold Traeger

Claire McLellan

Eva Prokop

Lee-Ann Patterson

Tom Lee

Raymond Meyer

Kevin McMullan

Kately Brown

Daniela Tadé

Kevin McMullan

Kevin McMullan

Paul Dickson

Kevin McMullan

Cia Parker

Liz Spruit

Staticgirl

Bradley Hutchteman

Gary Ussery

Illias Katsouras

Steven Barker

Ela Kowalczyk

Ela Kowalczyk

Ela Kowalczyk

Ela Kowalczyk

Meg Price

Carla Knopperts van Wijk

Shirley Mei

Robert Thomas

Peter Hasselbom

Pascal Ridel

Hideaki Kondo

Susan Howard

Maasje

Jolanta Kucharska

Voldemar Zubariev

Meg Price

Ian McMonagle

Derek Lasen

Susan Flyod

Ellen

Michelle Silze

Chris Isherwood

Tina Weber

Carol MacKinnon Ball

Howard Mitchell

Fraser Agar

Aaron D. McCormick

Leonora Enking

Jess Freeman

Kerri Lee Smith